Exercise

WAYLAND

First published in 2008
by Wayland

Copyright © Wayland 2008

Wayland
338 Euston Road
London NW1 3BH

Wayland Australia
Level 17/207 Kent Street
Sydney NSW 2000

Senior Editor: Jennifer Schofield
Designer: Sophie Pelham
Digital Colour: Carl Gordon

CIP data:
Gogerly, Liz
   Exercise. - (Looking after me)
   1. Exercise - Juvenile literature 2. Exercise -
   Physiological aspects - Juvenile literature
   I. Title
   613.7'1

ISBN: 978 0 7502 5308 6
Printed in China

Wayland is a division of Hachette Children's Books,
an Hachette Livre UK company.

Looking After Me

Exercise

Written by Liz Gogerly
Illustrated by Mike Gordon

WAYLAND

We love playing with our grandma. She's not like any other Grandmother. She's fast on her feet.

4

She's as strong as an ox

and she's very bendy, too – just watch her stretch.

Why is grandma so fit?
What's her secret?

When she was little, they didn't have television, so they did lots of other things instead.

In those days, children always walked to school. They enjoyed the fresh air and they met their friends along the way.

When grandma was at school, children played more sport.

At home, there were always jobs to do.

Even though she's old now, Grandma still likes to exercise. She told us that it's important that we exercise, too.

When grandma came to visit, she said, "Don't be a couch potato. Switch off the TV! Put the games away!"

11

Grandma told us that exercise is good for your heart and lungs. It keeps you fit and strong, too.

She said that helping around
the house is exercise, too.

14

It can be lots of fun

and just as good for you
as working out!

Grandma took us on
a scooter ride.

Isn't this fun?

Then we went
swimming.

She was amazing!

That night we felt really tired.

We slept so well.

The next morning, we felt happy and full of energy.

Now we have found lots
of ways to fit exercise
into our day.

We like to walk, cycle
or skateboard to school.

At school, we play games
during break.

Sometimes, after school, we play some sport.

Emily is fantastic at gymnastics. She's joined the netball team and has made lots of new friends.

Tom is terrific at tennis...

and he's captain of the football team.

At other times we go to the park to play hide and seek.

As a treat at the weekend,
we go to 'Monkey Business'.
It's like a gym, but it's just for
kids. It has slides, bouncy castles,
trampolines and ball pools.

We like exercising so much that we've got mum and dad doing it, too.
Now we go on bike rides together.

Or for a walk in the woods.

We've discovered something else...
Exercise doesn't have to feel like exercise.

As long as it's fun, it doesn't matter how you get fit.

NOTES FOR PARENTS AND TEACHERS

SUGGESTIONS FOR READING **LOOKING AFTER ME: EXERCISE** WITH CHILDREN

Exercise is the story of twins, Emily and Tom. With the help of their super-fit grandmother, they discover that you need to exercise to keep fit and healthy. The story begins with a visit from their grandmother. Emily and Tom obviously love her company and enjoy listening to what life was like when she was younger. Most children can identify with this relationship with a grandparent or older relative or family friend. You could ask the children about the older people they know. You could suggest they talk to this person about exercise and keeping fit when they were young. This would be a good way of setting up a discussion comparing ways of keeping fit now and in the past.

Today, lack of exercise is often a result of watching too much television and spending long periods of time on computers and on games consoles. Like many children their age, the twins enjoy watching television and playing computer games and it is their grandmother who suggests they look for other things to do. This would be a good opportunity to talk to the children about their own daily habits. Do they think they watch too much television? Do they play computer games? What kinds of exercise do they do? Which new activities would they like to try? By reading on, and looking closely at the illustrations, children will discover lots of interesting and possibly new ways of exercising. Did they ever think that cleaning, working in the garden, dancing or walking were forms of exercise?

The story shows that exercising can be fun and it can bring us many more benefits than just keeping fit. For example, Emily and Tom make more friends when they play team sports, such as netball and football. As captain of the football team, Tom will learn leadership skills, too. Can the children think of other benefits from exercising?

LOOKING AFTER ME AND THE NATIONAL CURRICULUM

The Looking After Me series of books is aimed at children studying PSHE at Key Stage 1. In the section *Knowledge, Skills and Understanding: Developing a Healthy, Safer Lifestyle* of the National Curriculum, it is stated that pupils are expected to 'learn about themselves as developing individuals and as members of their communities, building on their own experiences and on the early learning goals for personal, social and emotional development.' Children are expected to learn:

• how to make simple choices that improve their health and well-being to maintain personal hygiene;

• how some diseases spread and can be controlled;

• about the process of growing from young to old and how people's needs change;

• the names of the main parts of the body;

• that all household products, including medicines, can be harmful if not used properly;

• rules for, and ways of, keeping safe, including basic road safety, and about people who can help them to stay safe.

BOOKS TO READ

Walk Like a Bear, Stand Like a Tree, Run Like Wind Carol Bassett
and Clare Amy (Nubod Concepts, 2003)
Little Yoga by Rebecca Whitford (Hutchinson Children's Books, 2005)

ACTIVITY

Exercise Charades

This is a great guessing game that the whole class or a group of children can play. Each child in the group needs to think of a sport or any form of exercise. Then they take it in turns to act out this activity. The person who guesses correctly becomes the next person to act out their chosen activity.

INDEX